What people say about

"My dear friend your poem is very ... derness for your lover and yet you ... duty, to follow. You should chose ... battle with you in the poem. I wou ... ...an in love that everything we do in helping humanity, we do together. Forgive me I am too sentimental "

- **Sergio Ortiz**
Teacher, Philosopher, Poet and Artist
San Juan, Puerto Rico on "Farewell, my love"

"Saswati, thanks for this poem. I was getting despaired and dispirited these days due to dismal condition of communist movement. But your poem has filled me with enthusiasm and courage to fight the system and obviate in justice.

Though the architecture and style of poem is simple but it has immense underlying aesthetics which appeals the deeper cores of existence... This one is very, very, very BOLD poem... BIG BRAVO to you.
Muktibodh famous poet of Hindi wrote..
Todane hi honge garh aur math sab
uthane hi honge Aviwayakti ke kahtre
(Must be bulldozed these citadel of mighty injustice
We must afford Risk of Expressing the truth)"

- **Ramdahin Misra**
Activist from Kolkata on "Freedom of Humanity"

"Simply wonderful. It says it all in the back cover synopsis. Many things attracted me to this book, the cover for one. Very nicely done. The cover was actually painted by Saswati's husband Biplab Chattopadhyay. I love it. Saswati does a great job in really showing love, innocence, pain in her poems. As well as showing the ugly and unscrupulous side. Very well done Saswati. Here is an excerpt of my favorite:

Insane
I may use a thousand words to define me,
But all will go in vain-
At the end of the day, should I say,-

You will simply call me insane.
I fear not being named so,
I dare take the stride-
All the conventional rules
I simply refuse to abide."

-Ashton
Book Reviewer

"A great work. I liked these lines a lot:
I am the toil of a farmer;
I am honesty which is unsold,
I am the principles you uphold'
Good flow of thoughts."

-Matangi Mawley
Poetess and writer from Tamil Nadu, India
on "I am the song of humanity"

"Nice poem. Excellent choice of words!"

-Indrajit Mukherjee
Blogger from Cleveland, OH on "Love"

"Very Fresh and Inspiring Poem"

-Jalaja K Marella
Software Specialist, IBM Global Services,
on "March for a Grand Victory"

"Excellent poem - i loved it "

-Kamakhya
Blogger on "Let thy love be my inspiration"

"Just amazing work!"

-Manik Joshi
Poet from Pune, India

Fragrant Flute of Fire

Poems on
love…life…Revolution

Saswati Das

Fragrant Flute of fire

Copyright © 2011 by Saswati Das

All rights reserved. No part of this book may be reproduced or transmitted in any form or by any means without written permission of the author.

ISBN 978-0-9834102-7-0

Library of Congress Control Number: 2011903346

Published by
Biplab Chattopadhyay,
10635 Granby Way,
San Diego, CA- 92126

Cover Design by Biplab Chattopadhyay

Edited by Sri Sankar Kumar Das

Visit the website www.saswatidas.com for more information and suggestions.

Dedicated in fond memory to my grandfather
Sri Kabindranath Das

Acknowledgments

The process of writing this book of poems traces back to my adolescent days when I started developing a passion for poetry. From those good old days to this, I have platoons of people to thank for their undeniable contribution in one form or the other. First of all, I want to thank this life which has exposed me to the myriads of experiences, emotions, circumstances and people which has urged me to put my feelings into rhymes. I wish to express my gratitude to my grandfather, Late Kabindranath Das, who instilled in me a love for poetry. I wish to thank my parents, Sri Sankar Kumar Das and Smti. Basanti Das, for creating an ideal environment of altruism necessary for a poet's heart to grow. I would like to thank my friends in my school, colleges, universities and my neighborhood both in India and US, who have always loved my poems, admired my creation, provided useful remarks to improvise them, gave me opportunities to recite my poetries in socio-cultural gatherings and encouraged me to publicize them so that it touches the lives of millions of people. Among them includes Abhijit Banerjee, Bibhas Mitra, Monikonkona Sharma, Arnab Banerjee, Carol Conway,

Amit Parkhe, Subhas Beerge, Sunil Ghate and Mousumi Das, to name just a few. A special mention needs to be made to my best friends Afia Begum, Papri Maity, Appu Kumar, Vishal Roy, Banasri Sarkar and Sejal Sawalkar for their continued inspiration in the whole process. I am grateful to all my well-wishers both known and un-known who have written kind words of appreciation in my blog, some of which are listed in the testimonial section. I owe a lot to my aunts Bijoya Deb and Deepti Deb for their inputs on my creation and providing me the much needed information about the publication industry in India. I am especially thankful to my husband Biplab Chattopadhyay for painting the cover page and taking initiative in the publishing process. I would also like to express my gratitude to my friend Ramon Kabir for providing thoughtful inputs in designing the cover page and to Gargee Chattopadhyay for her sincere support. A personal thank you goes to my father for editing my composition and providing valuable inputs in designing the format of the book. I am fortunate to have a brother like Sri Sohanjyoti Das who took an active role in the advertisement of the book. I am grateful to my parents-in-law Namita Chatterjee and Sibsadhan Chatterjee for providing me the motivation and sister Vishakha, brother Sourav, uncle Nikhil Mukherjee and my cousins for their assistance in publication and marketing. I cannot complete this acknowledgement section without thanking the Createspace team for providing such a user-friendly tool and thereby making book publishing a painless process. Last but not the least I would like to thank the readers for without you, the fragrance of this flute cannot last long.

Preface

"Fragrant flute of fire" is not just meant for the poets, writers, thinkers, literary giants and philosophers. It is for common people with their joys and sorrows, pains, hopes, loneliness, love, grievances and continuous struggle for existence. It has been my earnest effort to find light and spread beauty in the less beautiful corners of world. From romance to revolution, from frustrations to hope, from friendship to solitude, from fearfulness to bravery, from oppression to revolt, my poems have tried to touch the varied emotions it has come across during its brief existence. It has spoken of love and the pain that dwells in life and earned accolades from the youths. It has spoken of corruption, struggle, division among people, riots and injustice in the society and could not stir hearts to fight against it. Finally it has blend romance with revolution, love with universal affection, hope with pain, joy with selflessness and found its real purpose on this world.

My poetry speaks of beauty, nature, romance and bliss. It loves to rhyme and sing and add melody to its lines so that it can evoke people's emotion and touch the hearts of audience. But simply dealing with beauty is not its goal. Its purpose is to commute the serious aspects of life, to highlight the grievances of the people, to inspire youths to fight against the evils of the society. Its purpose is social though its appeal is personal. The writer in me has found its meaning in transmuting pain to poetry. If my poems can touch the reader's heart, if audiences can identify themselves with my rhythm, if my peoples' emotions can find their voices in my poetry, if my verses can urge the youths to fight against injustice, if the melody of my flute can eliminate fear from a trembling soul, if a frustrated brother can find rays of hope in the darkness through my lines, if an unfortunate sister rise up in revolt against oppression through my words, if my song can help a wandering soul find a purpose in life, if my poems can stir young hearts to action, if my poetry can inspire a revolution, only then I will believe that my writing has been successful.

Table of Contents

Valentine's Day	1
Call for a Revolution	3
Struggle for Liberty	5
Farewell my love	6
Radiant Rays of Love	8
Traveler	9
Love my song	11
Personality	12
You came to my life	13
Love	14
March for a Grand Victory	15
Beauty	16
Freedom of Humanity	17
As you go away	18
Insane	19
Worthful life	20
Let thy love be my Inspiration	21
I am the song of humanity	22
Nobody else will	23
Bondage	24
In the silence of thee	26
Labour Law	27
Loneliness	29
Public Opinion	31
Love Unexpressed	32
Happiness	33
Preference	34

I think	35
Innocence	36
Real and Ideal	37
Perfection	38
Wishes	39
On love	40
Pain	41
Hope	42
Truth	43
Sublimity	44
I owe	45
How much I do care	46
A fighter I am	47
Bring back those days to me	49
To a parting friend	51
An Infatuation	52
You do not exist	54
Song from a deserted soul	55
Shadow	56
Struggle	57
Goodbye	58
Thee	59
To a proposal	60
Sacrifice	62

Valentine's Day

Tell me, Oh my Valentine,
How do I wish thee!

When the world is full of sores and pains,
When the days are long devoid of rains,
When beside me crawl exploiters
Of cold blooded veins,
Unbound and free-
Tell me, Oh my Valentine,
How do I wish thee!

With what flowers do I tribute
When there are thorns, thorns all while,
When the child at my next door
Has forgotten her smile,
When for bread and cloth, women have
Their self- esteem to pay,
Tell me, Oh my Valentine,
How do celebrate the day!

How do I celebrate the night
With chicken roasted red,
When hungry children cry all the night
For a single piece of bread,
When a jobless brother in frustrations
Has to take the gun in hand,
Tell me, how I roam with thee
In gay hand in hand!

When the lanes of my childhood
Are devoid of bird's song,
When drops of blood appear in the garden
Of flower and corn,
When stronger ones exploit the weak
And make them live in mourn,
Tell me, how I celebrate
The Valentine's Day dawn!

Go, go my valentine,
Come not me near,
My life has been darkened by
My people's grief and fear-

Perhaps in some other life,
I would be born to see,
My people free from fear and grief,
Playing in the world with glee-

On that day my Valentine,
We'll all laugh and enjoy,
By singing songs of liberty,
Love and joy!

Call for a Revolution

When the heart no more could comply with the bounds
When fears could not dismay
When the chains couldn't bind the soul
Of the fighters to proceed in the way.

Freedom, freedom was the song of the soul,
Freedom, freedom in the sky,
Struggle, struggle was the call of the day
Struggle for you and I.

One bird rose with the song of the soul
It was shot by the oppressor's gun
But while dying his melancholy strain
Called millions to join the run.

From each drop of that fell on the soil
From the heart of the dying bird,
Another bird rose up
And the cry for liberty was heard.

Millions laid down their life
And rivers of blood flowed by,
And then finally the stars of freedom
Were found to shine in the sky.

Freedom now is in the song of the child
Freedom among youth and old,
But misconceived freedom made man reckless
And oblivious of the principles they should hold.

Corruption crept into the life blood,
Fraternity gave its way,
Once again the killings of innocent lives,
Shaded the shine of the day.

Injustice against the weak and the poor
Has culminated human rights,
Exploitation and class distinction
Has come to the limelight.

Once again is the need of a total change,
Listen to the call of a revolution,
Do the youths of today have the guts
To take up the flag of mission.

Who has the courage to take the lead,
Ready to risk the life;
To make the world a better place
For the posterity to survive?

Struggle for Liberty

Oh listen, listen to the voice,
For there the cuckoo cry;
We'll have to sail through the ocean of blood-
For the deep blue sky.

Here's misery and whips of tyranny,
Pains, pathos outcry-
There the bird of liberty and freedom
Throughout the day fly.

Exploit us they, our feet being chained
But amidst darkness, the candle still flames-
Every drop of blood that runs through the veins
Sings, Sings and says again-
Thousands of sacrifices is the demand of the day
Fight we must, though die we may.

Such victory always summon blood-bath and martyrdom
Let's measure the nights of death and sacrifice,
The brilliant sun there arise-
To heel our hurts and charm souls with gaiety
By the songs of justice and liberty.

Farewell my love

Love though ye, oh my love
Loved in the dark and shine,
Love though ye, oh my love
I can't stay being thine.

When the voice of duty calls
Bind me not by love-enthralls,
Touch me not by plaintive words
For self is not now mine.

Love though ye, oh my love
Loved in the dark and shine,
Love though ye, oh my love
I can't stay being thine.

Far across the mountains and sands
The enemy's troop captures the land,
I'll go there to free the Mother
Look, she beckons in sigh.

Love though ye, oh my love
Loved in the dark and shine,
Love though ye, oh my love
I can't stay being thine.

Come I may, but go I must
To give the blood and quench the thirst,
Of miles long hot dry dust
Be weather foul or fine.

Love though ye, oh my love
Loved in the dark and shine,
Love though ye, oh my love
I can't stay being thine.

If I come back, oh my love, with glory to the goal
You and I will forever be united by the soul,
But if I kiss death, oh my dear
Insult not love by frustrating tears,
For my soul will love thee always
Love in the dark and shine,
My memories will inspire thee
And always remain thine.

Let the world know, our love is not
Just an illusive infatuation,
Let the world know it is but
A perennial source of inspiration;
Which liberates the mind and illumines the soul
And inspire heart towards great goal;
Which sacrifices itself unselfishly
When called for the sake of humanity,
And thus shows the world with brilliance
Its ever-radiating sublime beauty.

Radiant Rays of Love

I know not how the radiant rays of your love
Come to me
Through some unseen unknown trackless channels
In the form of inspiration for life-
They touch deep into my soul
And flow through my veins
They surround me like the brilliant sunshine
And give me a freedom illumined.

Traveler

*I traveled through the mountains,
I traveled through the wood;
I wandered through the forest
As far as I could-*

*I sailed through the rivers
I breathed in the sea
I tried to touch the horizon
As far I could see-*

*I climbed the skyscrapers
And the lofty tower
I saw the brilliance
Of the cruel power;*

*Roaming through the world,
As my traveler cease-
Nowhere nowhere
Could I found peace-*

*And then finally
I went to city
To slum, to village
To people's simplicity*

*I saw their struggle
Their weakness and strength-
Their pain and misery
What all they meant-*

I empathized with them
And their trembling faith
I supported them
In their eternal gait-

I fought for their rights
I felt their smiles
And with them, through them
As I walked for miles-

Suddenly I realized
I found peace
The unrest of my heart
Now cease to exist-

My wandering heart
Have found the nest
And this is the place
I travelth best-

For nothing is more wondrous
Than the human
Their life's a story
As deep as ocean-

And here I belong
After all I roam
My traveler's heart
Finds a home-

Love my song

Love my song and not me
Oh, friend of my soul, goodbye-
You will not know to compose a pain
How many tears role by!

Far there, on a flower garden
Sang a bird all day;
The song all heard, yet forgot the bird
Who at the dusk flew away.

I am but a wandering cloud
Travelling from land to land;
But my poems will share your heart
And inspire you till the end.

And then one day, on a calm spring dusk
Long after I am gone;
Share our tales with a caring friend-
For the sake of a song, unsung.

Personality

Illumine the world around you
By the brilliance of your personality;
So that when you leave the world
Cry the entire humanity.

If someone doesn't cry for you
If no-one listens
Do what your heart says right
Where conscience does not question!

The world is made by those few
Who knows to refute,
Only the brave can dare defy
When the rest remains mute!

You came to my life

Like a storm you came to my life
And revolutionized my inner self,
I realized a dream far beyond
Worldly joy, pleasures or pelf.

A dream that was to transform myself
A truth of life I had never known;
From illusion to knowledge, from fear to freedom
A ray of light, you have shown.

My imagination got flared up
By the blaze of your ideal;
I discovered myself waking from slumber
Into a world, genuine and real.

Your burning instance gave me the zeal
And an ever-illuminating inspiration;
With that courage, I voyaged on a journey
Ahead to the goal of perfection.

You showed me the path and I proceeded
To know in the world, my real worth
With unflinching faith and undaunted spirit
Towards absolute bliss and eternal mirth.

Love

My love is pathosful,
Yet serene and full-bloom;
It lays me down at the bed of thorns,
Then renders me immune;

A love that beckons-
A truth that touches;
A psalm that sings of purple glow-

Melancholy strain and plaintive notes though
Touches every heart to the core;
Yet at the end, there's the thunderous blow
Of hope, strength, struggle and fight.
For a joy eternal and infinite-
In a soul bathed in the morning sun
At the highest zone of virginal light.

March for a Grand Victory

Oh my heart, take me to the zone of light-
Where there is no moan, no plight;
Where the eyes can see beyond the horizon
Of private joy and selfish pride.

Where the song of soul is freedom
Freedom from illusion and cowardice;
Where in the eternal fight of life
Virtue prevails over the vice.

A mount from where the ears can hear
The pithiest call of the suffering millions-
And the feet can run to mingle-
In the ocean of mankind, at one summon.

I need, I need the courage and the strength
Nay, Nay, I lack it no more-
For the mind has awakened and spirit imbibed,
And time is knocking at the door.

The hour of final onslaught had struck
And I am ready with sword sharpened;
To cut the chains and break the walls
Ahead for a Victory, Tremendous and Grand.

Beauty

Full with joy my heart fills
When you bloom like the daffodils;
In the morning sun, with a smile that heels-
The pains of all and all evil ruins
The goodness of your nature falls,
Over one and all whoever calls;
And I am bound to say in winter or spring
A calm bliss that your presence bring,
Through the clouds that float over mountain tops
In secret silence;
Your heart that speaks and soul that sings
Has always something in its deeper sense-
A peaceful dream, a love serene,
A tint of pure innocence.

Freedom of Humanity

Amidst the hunger and amidst cold
Will rise the army in unity;
The workers, peasants and exploited class
Ahead for the freedom of humanity.

With the Red flag in the hand
And sprit of sacrifice in soul,
To protest against the injustice
And march towards the eternal goal.

A world of freedom and equality
Is the dream of the proletariat,
'Equal share for equal work'
And co-operation in people's trait.

The night is now not too long,
Beyond horizon, I hear an ocean's song;
For the mass have awakened in unison-
They shrink no more, they fear no more
To bring about a revolution.

As you go away

I remained watching the lonely way
Through the dry leaves as ye go away,
You looked not back nor made reply
Days passed by and by;

I waited for thee
A whole night long,
If you come to me
Even in the dawn.

But I know not why
Wait ended not,
May be friend
You forgot,-

The days we passed
The song we sang,
All those ended
In a short span;

I thought one day,
You would come along,
Through the same lone path
After a short sojourn;

One tear fell, then became dry
Void inside me, like the vast blue sky,
Asked so many questions in deep silence
That echoed back to me;
You never came, you never knew,-
I remained waiting for thee.

Insane

I may use a thousand words to define me,
But all will go in vain-
At the end of the day, should I say,-
You will simply call me insane.

I fear not being named so,
I dare take the stride-
All the conventional rules
I simply refuse to abide.

I choose to lead life that way
I care not being left alone,
So what if I have to die,
Unheard-unsung-unknown.

I break and shatter all the bounds
I prefer to be recklessly free
Like a wild wind I move
And invest for life in spree.

Worthful life

Wed my thoughts with thy ideals
Illumine my soul by thou sublimity;
So that a life worthful I live
And prove useful to the humanity.

Let thy love be my Inspiration

I aspire thy love which comes to me
Through unseen paths not known,
It touches deep into my soul
Yet to the world not shown.

A love that circumscribes like the sunshine bright
And flows through the veins as a silent plight-
A love that asks nothing in return for all that one gives
A love that remains always beside far though it lives.

A love that is no infatuation
A love that knows no possession;
A love that means only sacrifice
And eliminates the pain
A love that remains always loyal
In sunlight or in rain.

A love that believes only in giving
A trust that adds life to my living;
A faith that guides from all vice
A feeling - innocent, serene and nice.

Let thy love come to me in such form oh dear-
So that it shakes off from my heart
All shame and all fear;
So that it brings me from dark
To ever-augmenting luminosity,
Let thy love inspire my life
Towards the height of sublimity.

I am the song of humanity

I am the smile in the face of a child,
Or the tears from the eyes of a bride;
I am the song of a cuckoo bird,
That herald the spring of hope and love;
I am the raindrops of the clouds that fly,
Or the longings when you say goodbye;
I am the freedom in the vast blue sky
I am the innocence when your babies cry;
I am the vastness of deep blue ocean,
I am the depth of your emotion;

I am the justice, for which you fight,
I am the sweat which is a worker's pride;
I am the song which you murmur,
I am the toil of a farmer;
I am honesty which is unsold,
I am the principles you uphold;
I am the truth, I am the vision,
You may sacrifice your life for which mission;

That which ties you all together,
I am that feeling of fraternity;
The joy that knows no selfishness-
I am that sense of equality;

Beyond the circumference of joy and moan,
I am that stage of tranquility;
The melody which sings of eternal love,
I am that song of humanity.

Nobody else will

There once lived a little girl who played with toys and balls;
She had stored in her room a bag full of dolls.

Once an old man came to her house and a question he posed,
"Of all the dolls that you have, which one, you love most?"

Out of the dolls - all gorgeous and sweet, she chose the ugliest one,
Ill-clad and with one leg broken, she told "It's this and none".

As the old man stood stunned, this did what she reveal-
"If I do not love this doll, nobody else will"

Bondage

In darkness and gloom I do remain
Ignorant of world's beauty,
Unknown of the power of knowledge
Devoid of childhood gaiety.

My dreams and joys were sold by parents
Only for a few coins,
To the group of unfortunate labour children
I was compelled to join.

Snatched from my mother's lap
I was sent under the master's whip,
To abide by what they dictate
And feed on what they give.

I know not what dreams are
And how the cuckoo sings,
I know not why the children run
When the school bell rings.

I know not the joys of sports
And glories of victory there,
In the game of life, I have been
Nothing, but a failure.

Destined to do heavy routine work
Is only my life's goal,
Added to that is injustice
Burdened upon my soul.

No! No! No more can I
Afford this compulsion,
I want to break the bounds
And march ahead towards my destination.

I want to fly like a bird in the vast blue sky
With wide wings of freedom,
And wonder about across the world
Of village, country and kingdom.

I want to be the king of my soul
And sing with the world together,
I too want to find my place on earth
Like you my brother!

In the silence of thee

Words, those never ending words,
Could they ever explain me-
Feel, feel deep in your heart,
And then you will know me.
The child lost within you,
I am that child in thee;
The dream that illumines your eyes,
I enlive that dream of thee-
Like a bird as you wander all about,
In the dusk do come to me,
Deep within, unknown to the world,
I dwell in the silence of thee.

Labour Law

Still today, even though
Implemented in the Labour law
Hardly do they follow
Decades after the May Day

As the struggle of our fore-fathers decay
Under the grave of fear
Listen listen, oh brothers
There is nobody to hear

People even do not know
There exists such a law
It's illegal to make one work
Beyond the hour eight

That minimum pay do exist
In law book the Great
Yet rarely implemented in our people's fate
This is such as much shame

That people are numbed and maimed
In the grave of fear
There is nobody to hear

The death silence still prevail
In the hypocritical cultural veil
As our nation derail
In the pomp and show of glamour

The Have-nots do clamor
And it goes to deaf ear
In the realm of fear

Fragrant Flute of Fire

Of ignorance, which reign
In the rat-race of the world
What did we do gain
It is only shame

Oh brother please hear
There is only a small life
Please do not fear

Loneliness

As I behold the drops outside
They peep through my window panes,
Deep inside some corner of my heart
I feel intense a lonely pain.

Lonely is my home so wide
So lonely are the lanes
Far above the lonely cloud
Shed pearl drops of rains.

Lonely is the cuckoo bird
All day who flies along
No one knows what pain is stored
In the melody of her song.

Away in the sea a lonely boat
Sails in the moonlit night
By and by it meets the horizon
And is lost beyond the sight.

Lonely always is the heart of a poet
Who writes the rhyme of life
In the melody of whose music
The soul of the world survive.

Lonely forever is the night's moon
Still it shines through field and hay,
And shows the path to some lonely travelers
In the dark, who lose their way.

Fragrant Flute of Fire

Gone are the days when we together
Used to dance and sing song,
But when loneliness is so spread all over
How can I be alone?

Public Opinion

Trust not in the thoughts of people
They vanish just as bubbles blow!
Strange acts by a common man are crazy
By a famous man, are trends to follow!!

Love Unexpressed

One day you might ask me
Why didn't I reveal my love to thee?
And still I won't answer, nor mention—
That true love needs no expression.

Happiness

No birds sing today in the sky
And no flower doth spring;
In the little garden of our yard
Which we had ploughed and grained.

The sunshine hath lost itself
In the darkest evening;
And we beneath that lonely tree
Hath tears to console and scream.

Still life goes on and on
For a hope survives in the living-
A gloomy night always summon
A bright sunny morning.

A gentle breeze after heavy shower
Is always pleasant and calm;
Just a moment's happiness can wipe away
An era of pain that's gone-

Thus says the holy soul
Thus says the wise,
Doth thus say the world's ways?
Doth thus say the life?

In the race of our earth
Only the strong is happy and blessed;
The weak perishes by and by
In the struggle for existence!

Preference

*I would prefer beauty to imperfection,
I would value more meaning than beauty;
I would chose purpose rather than meaning,
I compare not the useful to any entity.*

I think

Strength is no lack of kindness
Weakness is no compassion
Words gauge as much as deeds
Solitude is no salvation!

Innocence

It shines like a smile in the lips of a child
And glances like a pain in the eyes of a bride;
It shows itself in the love of a mother
And In the play of friends together.

It dwells in the height of selfless love
Which is higher and deeper than the sky above;
The patriotism of a soldier, his duty sense
Also tells the sublimity of innocence.

In this complex world of darkness and gloom
Like a shining star, it always bloom;
And above all gives the highest bliss
Of living a life simple, in peace.

Real and Ideal

*In my passionate pursuit for ideal love,
I failed to recognize real love-*

Fragrant Flute of Fire

Perfection

Perfection exists only in moments.
Let moments be made eternal.

Wishes

Life is not a bed of roses
And painful though it seems;
Man has the power to make it beautiful
And artful beyond all dreams.

The world can be yours for the taking
The only thing you have to do-
Is to keep going through the darkest nights
To make your dreams come true.

As you rise high, do look below
Help the unfortunates lying low;
Life's worth is gauged not
By pleasure or pelf,-
But the service for others
At the cost of self.

With affection, empathy and selfless love
Fulfill thy life's duty;
Prove yourself, give yourself
As a useful member of humanity.

I know not if you'll ever recall our love
I know not if you'll remember me-
My soul like a faraway star
Will always, always be with thee.

And when you reach the sky of honour
And sit in leisure in the morning dew;
Like a half-forgotten poem you'll know
Someone silently had prayed for you.

On love

The beauty of unrequited love is its incompleteness;
The beauty of requited love is its satisfaction.

Pain

Pain gives a purpose to live for;
Which happiness does suffer-

Hope

The flower has long withered away
No bee comes now near;
The song of bird now seems alien
Which once had been so dear!

The music of some flute unknown
Had been calling me from far away;
But now it has lost itself
In the din and bustle of the day.

Life doesn't dance in rhyme with nature
The soul nor sings its serene song;
Life-struggles had shown the bitter truth
To which I had been unknown so long.

But now longer the dreams and mirages
Can dissuade me away,
Nor does the tears of frustration
Distract me from the way.

I'll embrace life with all its tastes-
Sweet, bitter or sour;
I'll fight and fight and attain my goal
And one day bliss with shower.

The withered flower will once again blossom,
And bees will come to meet;
The song of bird will please the soul
And flute's music will greet.

Truth

*We all know, we all feel
Truth may not always triumph;
Few know – guts to follow the truth
Is far more rewarding than triumph.*

Sublimity

*Often love gives us an opportunity to rise to sublimity;
Few take this and glorify love.*

I owe

I do not know,
To thee how much I owe,
But I must acknowledge, I know
If you weren't in my life
I wouldn't have been
What I am or where I survive.
May be in some dark lane, lone and bare
Seeking destination everywhere,
And yet moving away from it
In every movement of the feet.

How much I do care

In the voidness of my solitude
In my deepest prayer;
My silence could not divulge
For thee, how much I do care.

A fighter I am

Pain thou have given to the soul
I complain not a word to thee,
But give me the strength, so that I can
Endure the grief ye have given to me.

Thorns thou have sowed in the way
For me to tread on,
Give me the courage, in the route of duty
So that I may go on.

Let the feet be flooded with blood
And the brows with perspiration,
Still I may proceed in life
Give me that inspiration.

Thy mirages in the world, when tempts the heart
With futile dreams and illusions,
Give me the strength so that I can
Overcome all detractions.

Worldly ties of joy and moan
When surround the life and bind the soul,
Give me the zeal to free myself
And march towards my goal;
So that in the world stage
I may play my true role.

Let me survive the rumour beside
And thwarting failures from all side,
So that I may march ahead
With the flag of mission in hand,
And in the course of time
I may pay my debt to the land.

Let the rays of your love surround me
And make all my nights shine
Such that the life thou have given to me
I may make it sublime.

Bring back those days to me

A child I was, loved to play
And sing with birds of sky,
Snatched from the nature, I was thrown
Into the competitive world to strive.

In this man-made world of struggle
The fittest only survive
I too became materialistic
In my views of life.

Away from love and esthetic joy
That exists in the lap of nature,
I joined a world of competition
Where mutual rivalry is a culture.

I learnt to be envy of my fellow friends,
Who go ahead in life,
To defeat them and win the race
Became my only purpose to survive.

Thus running after earthly gains
Of name, fame and pelf;
Eventually I lost myself
Of my real self.

Years after this futile race
For fame and power;
Finally I succeeded to achieve
All that I desire.

Now I have a luxurious life
Name and wealth do shower;
But no real friend, with whom I can
Joys of success, share.

I know not how I got isolated
For the world nearby,
I know not how my ears deafened
To the strains of human cry.

Money gave me worldly status,
Position, comfort and pleasure;
Not the content of a worthful life
And peace of mind to treasure.

No one to cry on my pain
No one to smile at my gain;
No one to be my inspiration
In the path of my life.
No one to support in my endeavours
For all that I strive.

Oh, bring me back my childhood song
Bring me the days that are gone;
Give me the joy with which in nature
I use play, laugh and run.

Give me the love, I had for the world
Give me the bliss of soul;
Oh, now I realize- sharing love with people
Is life's real goal.

To a parting friend

Through dark nights of cloud and rain
When fake friends do flee;
Oh my friend, oh dear my friend
You had always been near me.

Like a strong pillar of support
You always stood by me;
Always lifting, always inspiring
You had been there for me.

A smiling face, an honest heart
An unflinching faith for the God above;
With so many credits at your treasure
Your very presence is a source of pleasure.

I know not how to spend my nights
Of stormy tears and lonely frights;
Without you, oh my dear friend
Sans your ever-compassionate hand.

In life journey, from end to start
Men meet and men depart
But pals like you stay in heart
Forever, forever a day.
The world is a small place
So we will meet some day.

For that day, oh dear buddy
I will wait for thee;
Hope till that date of life
You will remember me.

An Infatuation

Oh friend, thy love was no inspiration
It was merely an infatuation
An elusive attachment
A transitory phase-
Which comes and goes in life's long race.
Shows the eyes a few false dreams
A horizon of beauty though it seems
But no realistic touch of love and joy
Or glimpse of light in dark and void
An encouragement for which I always aspire
In tears and moan, to which I may retire
In the path of work, that do inspire
To reach new heights
Leaving all plights;
That retracts to the route of duty
A love that illumines life
Towards worthful beauty.

It was no boost to me
To become a real man;
It did never support me
To do what I can.

Just as moonlight in lonely night
Glorifies life with rays
Oh friend, thy love never
Inspired to fight dark days.

The mission, I had chosen for me
The ideals of my life;
Thou had never cared to know
Or pray for what I strive.

So my friend I bid goodbye
With best wishes for thy life;
May thou one day know my ideal
And believe for what I strive.

You do not exist

From the date I knew myself
You had been near me;
Consoling in times of moan
And sharing the moments of glee.

In the path towards the goal
You had been a source of inspiration;
Your loving ways had encouraged me
To pursue towards perfection.

Across the distance of the vast space
Thou memories touch mine;
Thou name remains untarnished
Through rusting affect of time.

Every morning as thee make a prayer-
'May all my tears come to thee';
It wets my eyes with drops of pearl
How much you love me!

A sound in my yard woke me up
I found myself alone;
Like the spring days you were there;
And now you are gone.

Thy shadow mingled in the dawn
With the dizzy morning mist;
Oh friend you art a world to me,
You do not exist!

Song from a deserted soul

I saw a light in thy eyes
I thought that the world's all lights;
I knew not then thou art the best
The brightest of the brights.

I knew not then the shade is dark
And darker human heart;
I knew not that some eyes laugh
When some heart tears apart.

I knew not thy love was
The highest inspiration;
I knew not people also deal
For self- satisfaction.

So I searched all the night
In the dark among the stars;
I could not find the day's sun
Who had gone to enlighten others.

Perhaps that little part of thy love
Was all that stored for me;
But I will treasure it all my life
As a wonderful gift from thee.

Some people come in this world
To tell us how to live;
We know their value in our life
Only after they leave.

Shadow

You are like a shadow mine
Whom I am always trying to grasp
Yet missing every time.

But still it is there
In joys and moan
I know I know
You are my own.

You won't desert me
In the lone half way;
And will remain till my dark night
Finds its day.

If you were a real person
Would you've been like the shadow mine,
I fear, I fear the worldly matters
Would have tarnished thy love along the time.

I am glad you are just a shadow
Forever unchanged, forever mine;
Like the great God,
You are just a thought;
Too good to be true-
And hence sublime.

Struggle

Struggle, Struggle is the call of the day
Freedom, freedom is the song of the soul;
Sacrifice, the heart yearns for now-
Liberty is life's goal.

Goodbye

Let there be no tears to fall
Let there be no heart cry;
Let there be thy sweet smile in face-
When I say to thee, Goodbye.

Thee

In the dark hours of solitude
When no one does care;
When tears too roll by down the cheeks
Leaving the eyes bare-
In those moments of sob and cry
I have always found ye-
So my friend, oh dear my friend,
So much I love thee.

To a proposal

Show me not how smart you talk
Show me not your intelligence;
Boost not your graduate degrees
Reveal not your bank-balance.

Does it really matter?

Tell me how great a friend you are
Tell me how you kept promises;
Tell me for your last lost love
How much you made sacrifices.

Tell me about your idealism
Tell me the principles you uphold;
Tell me how in the world of bargain
Your honesty remained unsold.

Tell me how long did you wait
For a friend who said he'll come;
Tell me how to keep a relation
Hurdles you had overcome.

Tell me how kind you have been
When an enemy was in remorse;
Tell me how you forgive people
For their selfish discourse.

Tell me how you feel awful
For the plaintive world around;
Tell me how in spite of glories
You remain connected to the ground.

Tell me how much handsome is your heart
More than your appearance;
Tell me how you controlled yourself
From addiction and indulgence.

In those tales of your life
I may fall in love with thee;
And offer my heart and soul
Forever for ye.

Sacrifice

My heart became a barren land
My dreams became dry;
Yet the blaze of my sacrifice
Never lets me cry;

About the Author

Saswati Das was born in the beautiful city of Guwahati in Assam, India in 1980. Being very close to nature, she started writing poetry from the age of seven. Her inspiration to write has been her grandfather who instilled in her a love for verses ever since she had learned speaking. Composing poetry and recitation goes hand-in-hand with her as she believes 'Recitation gives life to poems'. Since childhood she has been reciting poems of the famous Nobel laureate Rabindranath Tagore in various Cultural Programs and has won many awards for it apart from accolades and appreciations from people. Inspired by her father, who is as a trade union leader of BSNLEU (Bharat Sanchar Nigam Limited Employees Union) and fights for the rights of laborers and workers, she started writing revolutionary poems since adolescence. Saswati has always been showered with lots of love and admiration from friends and well-wishers for her thought-provoking poetry adorned with romanticized recitation. Her poems have been published in the magazines of St. Stephen's High School, Cotton College, Assam Engineering College, and Bengali Association of Chicago and in the regional newspapers viz. The Assam Tribune, The Sentinel and Purbanchal Prohori. She has been the winner of poetry writing, recitation, and cultural performance competitions in Assam Engineering College, All Guwahati Bengali Poetry Association, Saradiyo Dispur Durga Puja Committee in Guwahati and has recited her poetry in the annual cultural events of State University of New York at Buffalo, Bharat Sanchar Nigam Ltd. and Rabindra Sammelan in Guwahati, and Bengali Association of Chicago.

Apart from poems, she also writes articles, practices martial arts, loves reading non-fiction books, gets thrilled by travelling and takes part in social work. She did her Masters in Electrical Engineering from State University of New York at Buffalo and works as Senior Embedded Software Engineer in Navistar Inc. in Illinois. She lives in the historical city of Oak Park near Chicago.

Made in the USA
Charleston, SC
01 September 2016